Align to Love

Unlearning fear and aligning to love

Alexandrea Hicks

BALBOA.PRESS
A DIVISION OF HAY HOUSE

Balboa Press books may be ordered through booksellers or by contacting:

Balboa Press
A Division of Hay House
1663 Liberty Drive
Bloomington, IN 47403
www.balboapress.com
844-682-1282

Print information available on the last page.

ISBN: 978-1-9822-5237-3 (sc)
ISBN: 978-1-9822-5238-0 (e)

Balboa Press rev. date: 08/24/2020

Contents

Dedication

To my Angel; my cousin Stephanie Lee Hicks, it was always your dream to become a published author but God felt you needed your wings. The last we spoke we were planning to meet up for me to show you my ideas for this book. As I wrote this book, I felt your Spirit with me so strong every time I opened my computer and started writing, I know your Spirit was right here with me.

….When I think of you I think of a feather. Strong, flexible and free flowing in the wind just like your free spirit. I could only hope that anyone reading this will be able to feel that sense of free.

Your memory will live on in all of us.

Anois is arís

Hello Gorgeous!

Are you ready to shift out of fear and into a place of love? Chances are if you are reading this book then you are in a place of wanting to make a change in your life.

In this book you will find a daily guide to shifting out of fear and aligning to love. This book will help you to release your fears and to align to the vibration of love. This book will guide you to learn to LOVE you. It will guide you to let go of fear, to let go of worry, self- doubt, of anything and everything that makes you feel badly. I will be guiding you to get to a place of complete BLISS, and complete LOVE. We will cry together, laugh together, get creative together, write together. This is going to be a beautiful journey, and it can also bring up a lot of healing for you in the process. Embrace those moments, embrace the pain. Embrace the challenges that is what is allowing you to grow, allowing you to transform.

XO.

Letter to the old me:

Welcome to this beautiful journey, to shift and align you into the vibration of LOVE. I want you to write a letter to yourself. In this letter I would like you to include:

The date:

♥What are all of the old habits you are willing to give up?

♥Where is it you feel you need the most work?

♥What is it you want out of this journey?

♥What are you willing to do to get to where you want to be?

♥Will you commit every day?

knowing that you are in complete and total control of your thoughts and of how long you stay in a dark hole. Be aware, be conscious of it. Be conscious of your thoughts. When you're at work and something isn't going your way, or when you are arguing with your partner, instead of thinking that you're not good enough or that you could have done something to prevent the circumstances, just go back to the thought. "Today I choose the path of LOVE." When you make the conscious decision to choose the path of love, self-doubt, fear, and negativity cannot reside in the same place as love. Once you make the decision to choose the path of love, negativity will DROP out of your life.

I have a perfect example of this from my life. I said a prayer one day and the prayer was "I pray that anything that is blocking me from living life to my highest potential and anything that is not in my life for my highest and greatest good will be removed from my life. I said the prayer and a day later, one of my close friends dropped out of my life. At first I was upset about the circumstances, but to be honest I did not dwell there. The old me would have dwelled there probably for months. I felt the feelings and released it. I pictured her surrounded by white light, put her in a bubble, prayed for her, sent her love and blew the bubble away. I realized that I had prayed for everything to be released from my life that didn't serve me to my highest purpose. She just was not meant to be on my path anymore. It didn't mean she was a bad person, it just meant that she was no longer meant to align with me because I wanted to live in a place of love, and she was still living in a place of fear. The energies collided, so the Universe removed her from my life.

Love cannot live where fear resides. As you

focus on love and as you choose the path towards love, you will realize that many people will begin to drop out of your life. It is important for you to realize that this is completely acceptable, even when it hurts. Feel the feelings of anger or sadness but do not dwell in them; feel it then release it and then keep being true to you. Stay in your power. Stay in your love. Never lower yourself or lower your vibration to fit in someone else's life.

Choose Love.

Every damn day.

As you go through your day today, I want you to choose love. In every situation you are faced with. So when you're driving down the road and someone cuts you off, instead of flipping them off and yelling, just say I love you! (Not directly to them, just say it in your head or even out loud.) Just watch how different the energy will be if you do that. If you are having a difficult moment and having a hard time choosing the path of love, just look at what you wrote down earlier and choose to go right back to the vibration of love.

Evening Exercise:

Journal about how your experience went today.

❤Did you choose love?

❤Did you consciously try to change your mindset in any moment that you were thrown off by negativity?

❤Is there a situation that you wish you did handle differently today? If so write down exactly what you wish you had done, or said.

❤What are you most proud of yourself for doing today?

Repeat after me:

"I choose to see love instead of this. I will re align my energy back into the vibration of love by consciously choosing to think loving joyful thoughts instead of fearful thoughts."

Let Go..

Yesterday in choosing love a lot probably came up for you as far as what brings negative emotions to you. I want you to take a few minutes to sit down and take a few deep breaths in, close your eyes and just focus on your breath taking notice of how you're breathing. I want you to tune in to your feelings for a few moments and just sit in complete silence and just be present in the moment right now. As fearful thoughts enter your mind, I want you to write them down on a piece of paper. I also want you to take a few moments to think back to yesterday, to think back to any moment that made you fearful, or any moment that made you have negative thoughts.

❤Who were you around in these moments?

❤What were you doing in these moments?

❤What was it that triggered these negative thoughts?

These are all so important in the process of letting go. When we are in the process of letting go we must first be aware of exactly what it is that we are letting go of. Is it people? Is it the places we go? Is it our jobs? Is it our home lives? What exactly is it that is triggering bad feelings inside of us? Letting go is a process that we must go through over and over. We must shed all the layers in order to completely and fully release it.

Now this exercise can get a little emotional for you when doing it, because a lot might come up. I want you to sit in a comfortable space, set up a little area if you can, an area where you won't be disturbed an area that is your own little sacred space. You will be visiting this area a lot in this process while we are on this journey. Before you start writing I want you to cleanse your space, if you have sage light some sage. Light a white candle. Ask that you will be guided in this process to fully write down all that you need to release. Take a piece of paper and start writing what you are willing and ready to let go of. After everything that you are writing down, after it I want you to write…

"I am willing, and I am ready to release this for I have realized that this takes me out of the Vibration of love. I am ready to release this now and transform it to love and light."

I align with love.

Forgive Your Fears

The two F words. That can cause so many blocks in living life to our fullest potential.

Fear. Something that can cripple so many of us in life at times.

Forgiveness. Something that so many of us struggle with.

Sometimes it can be difficult to forgive. Many people find it challenging to forgive others for hurting us and even difficult to forgive ourselves for hurting ourselves, or for allowing others to hurt us. Forgiveness is one of the most powerful tools you can use on the journey to your true Self. Practicing forgiveness can release so many blocks in our lives and is so important on our journey to love.

I forgive you.

These three words can literally set you FREE. Forgiving your fears and forgiving yourself can change your life drastically. What exactly do I mean by forgiving your fears?

What I mean is, forgive all of the things that have held you back. Forgive yourself for allowing fear to hold you back at any point in your life. Forgive yourself for giving in to your fear.

What exactly is fear?

Fear is something that we create for no reason. We create fear because we think to ourselves all of the "what ifs". We create fear because we think of all of the things that could go wrong. Which then creates the things that go wrong because we've placed the fearful energy into it. You feel me? It is often said that the things we fear the most are the very things that happen to us. The reason being, is because our mind is so powerful so when we put the energy into our fears the law of attraction brings us just that.

Fear is, *FALSE EVIDENCE APPEARING REAL.*

Fear is, *FACING EVERYTHING AND RISING.*

Fear does not exist. All fear is, is a mental block that we have created in our minds to stop us from doing what we really want to do. Fear can be such an ugly thing, because it stops so many people from living in their truth, or from following their dreams. A lot of times we have fearful thoughts because we are afraid either that we are not good enough, or we are afraid that we are going to fail.

I want you to write down all of the things that you would do if fear wasn't in your way. Write them ALL down. Sit in your meditation space, take a few breaths, find your center, light some candles before you begin, and pause and just write. Whatever comes to you, write it down. Anything and everything that you would do if fear wasn't a factor in your life. Then I also want you to write after that what the fear is and why you believe that you cannot accomplish this. You will most likely start to see a pattern when you do this exercise.

Now, after you write your list, I want you to go back, and after each and everything that you wrote down. I want you to write,

"I'm sorry for allowing fear to block this, I love you, I forgive you"

Write this down…. Believe it. Feel it.

Feel the feelings of truly sending LOVE to the

situation and truly forgiving. In order to remove the blocks of fear, we have to send love to the blocks, and we have to forgive the blocks for appearing. I want you to really work with this throughout this day, and even throughout the week. Remember from Day 1, choose love. And for Day 2, we are letting go, Day 3 we are forgiving our fears and choosing to see love. Sending love to our fears, can help us to unblock the fears. It is just coming to a place of realizing that any of your fearful thoughts are not real.

Repeat After Me:

"I choose to send love to my fears, for I now know they are not real. I forgive myself for living fearful. I now am aware that I can consciously choose to think my way out of my fear based thoughts. As fearful thoughts enter my mind, I send them away with love. I choose to align with love."

Destroy Self Sabotaging Thoughts

Chances are, if you are anything like me on the path of self-discovery and self-love, when you saw this one, it sort of made you cringe. Yes, this is a hard one. Did you notice how I used the word DESTROY, and not RELEASE. We are not just releasing these thoughts. It is time to destroy them. Self-sabotaging is something that a lot of people struggle with.

"I am not good enough"

"I am not thin enough"

"I am not worthy"

This all sounds familiar, doesn't it? We ALL do this to ourselves at one point or another. The way to overcome this is to figure out WHERE these thoughts are coming from. Why are we telling ourselves we are unworthy and unlovable? Where is this coming from?

I want you to get out your journal and I want you to answer these few questions. Be completely honest with yourself, because this is what is going to help to heal you.

❤What do you believe is your biggest struggle with loving yourself?

❤Where do you believe this comes from?

❤How would you be different if you didn't have these thoughts?

❤What are you willing to do to get rid of these thoughts?

Then, I want you to write a letter to yourself. I want you to apologize to yourself for ever believing that you aren't good enough. I want you to apologize to yourself for ever telling yourself you are unworthy. Most importantly, I want you to apologize to yourself for ever allowing another person to make you feel unworthy, or like you were not good enough.

I want you to be mindful today- be mindful of your thoughts. When you have a self-sabotaging thought, where is it coming from? What are you doing in that moment that you are having this thought? Who are you with? What are you thinking about? It's so important to take notice of all of these details, because you want to see where these thoughts are coming from.

When we get these negative thoughts about ourselves, they aren't real. These thoughts usually come from someone else in our past making us feel unworthy or unlovable.

Repeat After Me:

"I choose to send love to all of my self-sabotaging thoughts. I now recognize that these negative thoughts that I have about myself are not real. I forgive myself for allowing this to overcome me in the past. I am now willing and ready to destroy my self-sabotaging thoughts once and for all."

Free Yourself

Today I want you to focus on the word FREE. I want you to focus on freeing yourself. When you think of the word free, what do you think of? How does that word make you feel? Does it bring you peace, does it bring you joy?

I want you to take out your journal, and write about how the word "free" makes you feel. Then I would also like you to write down the things that make you feel tied down. I want you to write down what makes you feel like you aren't free.

I want you to learn and to know that being free is a choice that we have every single day. You do not have to be stuck somewhere that doesn't make you feel good. This is all a choice. I want you to think about what being free would really be like to you. I want you to focus on that feeling all day today. Here is what I want you to free yourself from today. I want you to free yourself from the thought that you have to be a specific way for people to like you. I want you to free yourself from the fact that you can't be who you are because you are afraid of what other people will say. Speaking from personal experience, I went a long time in my life hiding who I truly was a person, because I was afraid of what other people would say or think of me. I spent so many years suffering from anxiety and depression because I was living completely against my truth of who I was. I decided one day, after hitting a complete rock bottom, that I was just going to be free and be me everyday for the rest of my life. Now, I am free to be me. I am not afraid to share who I am with people anymore, because truthfully when we aren't being our true selves, we hurt and feel a lot of pain. I want you to really focus on this today. I want you to be free, to be you. Free yourself from pain. Free yourself from being someone that you think you should be. Free yourself from having to look or act a certain way.

You are free to be you.
Write this down somewhere that you can take this with you today, keep it where you can see it often. You can even put it as a reminder in your phone so it goes off and you see it.

"I am free to be me."

Take your journal out and answer these questions.

❤Do you feel like you are truly living the life you wish to live?

❤Do you feel like you are living authentically?

❤Do you feel like you act a certain way to make others happy?

❤Are you willing to stop all of this to step into who you truly are?

❤What steps are you going to take to getting closer to being free?

Repeat After Me:

"I choose to live life freely. I choose to be me fully and completely. I choose to free myself from all pain and all suffering. I choose to free myself from thinking I should be better because right now in this moment, I am exactly where I need to be. And I choose to be free."

Get Rid of Expectations

Having expectations can cause us so much hurt and so much pain because when people or situations don't meet our expectations, we then feel hurt or upset about it. Today, I want to focus on getting rid of expectations. This could be a bit challenging because we are so used to living in a world where we often set expectations on friendships, relationships,our parents, even our work environment. Whatever the case may be, we tend to feel like people have to live up to what we want them to be or how they should be. This is a lot of times what causes us pain, especially in relationships. The thing with having expectations is that we are all coming from a different place, each and every one of us is in a different place within our journey. We all see things in a different light, we are all at different levels consciously. One of the best things to try to remember, is that each person in our life is acting in the best way that they know how for that moment. So when we get rid of the expectations in other people, it is like we are letting them off the hook. It is generally not the other people who hurt us on our paths, it is usually the expectations that we have for those people that truly hurt us. We all energetically, emotionally, and physically exist on a different level, so the way we see things sometimes others see it in a different light. I think it helps to always think that in any situation with another person, that they are doing the best that they can for where they are at on their journey in life. Remembering that has been something that has really helped the last few years. When you let go of expectations you are actually releasing yourself from being able to be hurt.

Get into your comfy space, light a candle, settle in to yourself.

Take your journal out and start writing.

❤Where is it that you are having too many expectations for yourself?

❤Where is it that you are having too many expectations for other people?

❤How has having expectations caused you hurt or sadness in your life?

Repeat After Me:

"I am now willing and ready to let go of having expectations. I realize that having expectations for other people will only cause me hurt and cause me pain and suffering. I understand that everyone is acting the best they can in the moment, the best that they know how. From this moment on, I will no longer have expectations for anyone or anything."

Become Willing

In order for us to align with the vibration of love, it is essential for us to become willing. Become willing to change old habits. Become willing to release all that no longer serves us for our highest and greatest good on our journey, on our path.

Are you ready and willing to let go of all your old beliefs? Are you ready to let go of old habits?

I want you to write a list here of all of the things that you are willing to become.

"I am willing to love myself"

"I am willing to manifest the life of my dreams"

"I am willing to let go of fears and doubts"

Write whatever it is that you are willing to do

and then next to it, I want you to write what you are willing to do to allow this to happen. For example: "I am willing to love myself."—Therefore every day I will do things that make me feel good and bring me joy. I will take the steps everyday to love myself. "I am willing to manifest the life of my dreams."—Therefore, I will write a list of all of the dreams and goals I have in life and promise myself everyday to take at least one step towards that dream. Make it your own. When you become willing, you are allowing yourself to be open to healing and to change old habits. When you become willing, you are opening yourself up for miracles to enter your life. We all have free will in life to choose our paths, so the first step to getting what you want is to become willing.

Repeat After Me:

"I am willing to let go of the old me. I am willing to let go of old bad habits, to create new healthy habits. I am willing to take action every single day towards bettering myself. Starting right now."

Feel Ya Shit

One of the biggest things in shifting and aligning to the vibration of love is to be able to feel all of our "shit" and process it. This is being able to feel all of the things that we have gone through in our lives that have made us uncomfortable, have hurt us, and caused us pain. In order to fully live in the vibration of love, we have to be able to feel these things, to heal these things. Unfortunately the only way to truly heal something is to actually feel the pain and sadness, and allow the feelings to release. This was one of the hardest things for me on my spiritual journey. There were days where I would want to just lay in bed and cry all day without even really knowing what I was crying about. The more you try and move into the light, the more that you have to feel all of the bad things. It's almost like a white light shining through your entire body and your emotional body. Anywhere that there is darkness the light will shine on to it, but in order for the darkness to go away and to fully allow the light in, you must feel what is coming up for you. A lot of times what is coming up for us is things that we have suppressed over the years and eventually you have no choice but to feel it. This can be uncomfortable, but it is what helps you to heal. This was truly one of the hardest things on my journey because I feel that many times in my life when something uncomfortable would happen to me, instead of really processing it, I would just block it out and move on with my life rather than actually sitting with the feelings of what was bothering me.

I'd like you to grab your journal, and write down these few things...get in your comfortable sacred place, light some candles, make some tea, grab your pen and let your heart guide you as you write on the pages.

I want you to just write. Without even thinking about what you're writing, just start writing what's been bothering you, or some things that may have happened to you in the past but you never really "felt" it. I want you to just start writing whatever comes out. If you're angry, express why. If you're sad, express why. Allow yourself to cry if you need to. This is what will help you release the stagnant energy, to clear your energy to allow the light to enter.

Repeat After Me:

"I am safe in the process of allowing myself to feel through my emotions. I am safe and I am loved. I recognize that this is just old, stagnant energy leaving my body and I surrender and allow these emotions to flow through me and out of me for good. I am safe and protected."

Face Your Shadows

A huge part of aligning to love is facing our shadows. You know, the dark pieces of ourselves. The parts that we do not like to talk about and sometimes try to suppress out of our lives. These parts must be healed in order to truly align into the vibration of love. So, I want you to take notice today of what triggers you. As you are going about your day, if something sets you off or makes you upset, I want you to really sit and think about what happened. Sometimes the littlest things can set us off, people we may not even know after an encounter in a grocery store, or even as we are in the car driving and someone makes us angry. Ask yourself- why did you get triggered by this? Usually when something makes us angry about another person it is because there is something that we see in them that we need to heal in ourselves. So for instance, say there is someone in your life that you feel like no matter what, they don't believe in you. Ask yourself, do I honestly believe in myself? Chances are this person is mirroring something that you need to heal, so the answer to this is you need to believe in yourself and when you believe in yourself enough you won't need anyone else to believe in you. Another example could be if you are in a relationship with someone and maybe you feel like they aren't giving you enough attention. Where are you not paying attention to yourself, and where are you not giving attention to yourself? Journal about this, and you will be so surprised at the healing that will take place when you finally realize what it is that is triggering you.

Repeat after me:

"I am ready to embrace my shadows and use my triggers to allow myself to heal. I now know and understand that whatever triggers me is bringing something to the surface for me to heal and it is safe for me to heal. I am safe and well"

Honor Your Space

(The big N-O)

My whole life I was always one of those people that said yes to everything, even if it didn't feel comfortable or "right" to me. I said yes to things that I didn't want to do and knowing I didn't want to do it I still said yes. Why? Most likely it is because we are so afraid of what others will think or say. I was always so afraid of people getting mad at me because I wouldn't do this or wouldn't do that. So I never honored myself, I would put others BEFORE myself, and it didn't feel good. It didn't bring me joy. If anything, it made me feel worse being stuck somewhere doing something that I didn't want to do.

Listen to these words I am about to lay down on this paper, because this is SO IMPORTANT on your journey....

It is okay to say NO.

Truly.

It really is okay to say no....

When something doesn't feel right, the answer is no. STOP saying yes to shit you hate. Stop saying yes to stuff you don't want to do. Stop saying yes to people who would not give the same in return. If something feels like a no, then say no. HONOR yourself. Honor your space. Honor your time. PLEASE, always, always honor yourself FIRST.

Today, I want you to pay attention to how many things you say yes to when it doesn't feel right. You will know, because you will instantly feel it. Then, I want you to practice saying no!

I have now come to a place in my life where I am always honoring myself first. People always joke with me that I am the worst at making plans, because I never know how I will feel that day, so if I wake up and I am not feeling it, the answer is no. If I don't want to do something I DON'T do it, and guess what? I am still living, and still breathing, nothing bad happened to me because I said no, crazy right? All it did for me was bring more positivity into my life. Say no to the things that don't bring you joy, and your ENTIRE life will SHIFT. I promise you this.

Repeat After Me:

"By choosing to live in the vibration of love, I realize that I need to only say yes to the things that excite my Soul. I will honor myself first, always. It is okay for me to say no to the things I don't want to do."

Shift Yo Vibes

To truly align with love, you need to be able to shift your vibration. On the path of aligning to love, it is so important to keep your energy positive and to keep your energy cleared. This also includes staying away from people who will bring your vibration down. When you are on the spiritual path and choosing love, you must stay away from anything giving you a negative vibration or feelings.

I choose to always align with love.

In order to keep your vibrations positive, you can practice grounding your energy. Some ways that you can ground your energy are: saging, using crystals such as black tourmaline, red jasper, tigers eye. Meditation can also help as well as taking a bath with epsom salt, or contact a Reiki practitioner to perform Reiki on you.

Grounding technique:

Close your eyes. And imagine that you are on a beach, your feet are in the sand, the warm sun is shining upon you and you feel the water gently flowing on your feet and as the water flows away from your feet carrying with it anything stuck or stagnant that no longer serves you. Just cleansing, and completely renewing you.

To Cleanse Energy:

To cleanse your energy there are a few different things you can do. You can light a white candle, you can burn sage. You can do a chakra clearing meditation. One thing that I love for clearing my energy is a salt bath. Something that works very quickly if you are out somewhere and you feel like the energy is not good for you, you can run your hands under cold water and just imagine the negative energy leaving your body. This is a great technique because you can pretty much do that anywhere. It might get a little weird if you just light up some sage in a public place, even though I am not going to lie, I've thought about that once or twice.

It's so important to keep in a positive vibration when you are on the spiritual path. It's so important to keep your space clear, get rid of clutter at home in your workplace. When you are trying to be in a positive vibration, you have to be able to receive energy. When you have clutter and chaos and negative energy around you, you will not be able to stay in a positive vibration.

Exercise:

Clear away the clutter from your home, your office, your car. Start getting rid of things that no longer serve your life. Stop holding on to things of the past. This isn't just a physical practice, this also resonates with your energy. When you are holding on to things that no longer serve you or don't bring you happiness, it will affect your vibration.

Also, take out your journal and start writing down the things that bring you happiness.

Who are you around when you feel your happiest?

Just allow yourself to let go and write whatever comes to you.

Lastly, I would like you to take note that you can feel this way all of the time if you take the steps to making the changes that need to be made in your life daily.

Repeat After Me:

"I choose today and every day to stay in a positive vibration. If anything comes into my life that doesn't serve me for my highest good, I let it go. I choose to only be in the positive vibration from this day forward. I choose to align with love, every single day."

Just Allow

An overwhelming feeling came over me as I was laying in my bed meditating. And I kept seeing the words...just allow. It really called me to start thinking about life and all of us in general how we tend to try and force things or control things based on what we think we want or what we think we need and what we think is best for us. Sometimes we try to control things so much that it actually messes up with the Universal flow. Life becomes so much more peaceful and you will become so much happier if you surrender, and just allow things to happen rather than trying to control everything. Think of it in this way: whatever the outcome of something is supposed to be, it will be, no matter how much you try to control it to be the way you think it should be. The universal law is if something isn't meant for you, it won't come to you. When you tend to place your energy into one thing and one thing only, you are blocking other things from coming and you could actually be blocking the very thing that IS meant for you. Think of a hose and the water is flowing but if you grab the hose too tightly, what happens? The flow gets stopped and it stops flowing through. This is exactly what happens when you don't just allow things to flow naturally. You are doing more damage than good because you are blocking the direct flow. Today, I want you to focus on just allowing things to flow. When you start to notice yourself trying to control something, stop yourself and say "I surrender, and I am just going to allow this situation to flow naturally."

Evening Exercise:

Take your journal out and answer these questions

❤Did you find yourself trying to control certain situations today?

❤If so, what were they?

❤How could you have handled it differently?

If you truly did stop yourself let go and allow that is absolutely wonderful.

Repeat after me:

"From this point forward I am going to stop trying to control things. I know and trust and believe everything is happening for my highest good in perfect and divine timing. I will let go, and just allow the Universe to do her thing. The Universe will give me this or something better, every single time."

Surrender To Your Faith

Faith is something that I always have had a strong belief in. No matter how hard things had gotten in my life, I always had Faith that better days would come. When I was younger, I suffered from SEVERE depression and anxiety. So bad that I was homeschooled for four years in high school. I was a walking panic attack, literally.

I also had a strong Faith, that someday things would get better.

I believe in life, that life really is what we make of it. I believe strongly and full heartedly in the law of attraction and the power of our thoughts to create our reality. Now this wasn't something that I always believed in. When I was in my severe depression, I honestly could never see a way out of it. I had wanted to give up more times than I could even imagine, but somehow I always kept going.

Faith is having complete trust in something without actually seeing the results, and oftentimes that can be challenging for a lot of people. We tend to get afraid to take risks in life because what if it doesn't work out the way we want it to? But, something that I have learned over the last few years is that we are in complete and total control of our lives and the outcome of our lives. We have to literally Faith it until we make it. We have to believe and have the faith in ourselves that our goals or our dreams ARE possible, because if you believe it then it will be possible.

To have Faith is to completely SURRENDER. Surrender to God, The Divine, The Universe, whatever it is that you believe in.

Surrender.

Stop trying to control, stop trying to force.

Surrender.

And trust.

Think of yourself driving in the car and you have your eyes on the road ahead of you. You cannot see your destination you can only see right in front of you, but you keep driving, trusting that as you continue to drive the road will continue and it will lead you to where you are going. That is what having Faith is. So keep your eyes on your destination, the end result, and allow the road to unfold ahead of you.

When you completely surrender and put your Faith to a higher power, that is when miracles occur.

Repeat after me:

"I fully let go and surrender to the Universe and the Divine and I know and trust that everything is unfolding for me in perfect and divine timing. I let go and allow miracles to occur."

My Wish For You

May you be able to find love all around you in all things, always. May you always know that no matter what you are going through, there is a lesson to come out of it, and the sunshine is on the other side of your pain and suffering. May you realize that you are capable of anything and everything that you put your mind to. May you forgive all of your fears, and take steps forward every day. May you surrender every day to your Faith. May you take the time to find your peace. May you see the light in you, and also in others. May you be able to align into the vibration of love and then also help others do the same.

"May you be as strong and

as free as a feather"

Printed in the United States
By Bookmasters